WHY ARE NATIONS AFRAID OF RED? THE RED SCARE

HISTORY BOOK OF FACTS

CHILDREN'S HISTORY

The words "Red Scare" were used when describing an intense anti-communism time period occurring in the U.S. The word "Red" stems from the Soviet Union flag color and the word "Scare" arose because people became scared communism would be coming to the U.S. In this book, you will be learning about the Red Scare and the events that led up to it, and people that were involved. The First Red Scare occurred after World War I and the Russian Revolution and the Second Red Scare took place after World War II, during the Cold War.

THE FIRST RED SCARE

Following the Russian Revolution in 1917, communism had become the first major form of government in Russia. Marxist Vladimir Lenin led the Bolshevik Party, leading the revolution. They were able overthrow the current government and they murdered the royal family. People were now not permitted to practice religion openly and the right to private ownership was taken from them under the communistic government. Many Americans became fearful that this form of government would overtake the United States.

VLADIMIR LENIN

COLUMBIA
DOC.
I.W.W
RED.

The first Red Scare took place from 1919 to 1920. Once the workers started to strike, many blamed communism. Several people were arrested simply because they were thought to have beliefs in communism. Under the Sedition Act of 1918, the government was able to deport people.

THE SECOND RED SCARE

The second Red Scare took place at the beginning of the Cold War and after the end of WWII. The second Red Scare lasted approximately ten years between 1947 and 1957.

COLD WAR MUSEUM

KOREAN WAR

Once communism started spreading in China and Eastern Europe, and with the Korean War, people feared that it could also infiltrate the U.S. In addition, the Soviet Union now had nuclear bombs and was known as a world superpower. People feared anyone that took the side of the communists and helped the Soviets obtain secret information about the U.S.

THE GOVERNMENT

The United States government was involved heavily with the Red Scare. Senator Joseph McCarthy was one of the major crusaders fighting against communism, and he was determined to oust them. He would use gossip and intimidation to obtain information and often did not have much evidence when he would accuse people of working for the Soviet Union and ruined the careers and lives of many people prior to Congress and other leaders bringing his actions to an end.

Led by anti-communist J. Edgar Hoover, the FBI got involved. They would spy and use wiretaps on people they thought to be communists and provide this information to McCarthy and the other anti-communist leaders.

RED SCARE POLITICAL CARTOON
U.S.
IMMIGRATION RESTRICTIONS
UNDESIRABLE

The House Committee on Un-American Activities was also involved in the Red Scare, this committee was a standing committee of the House of Representatives. Hollywood was one of the areas they investigated. Screenwriters, Hollywood executives, as well as directors were accused of being pro-communist. There were rumors that there was a Blacklist consisting of anyone that was suspected of associating with the American Communist Party and these people would not be hired during the Red Scare.

VLADIMIR LENIN

Vladimir Lenin was the Chairman of the Soviet Union. He was born in Simbirsk, Russian Empire on April 22, 1870 and died at Gorki, Soviet Union on January 21, 1924. He is best known for being the leader of the Russian Revolution and establishing the Soviet Union.

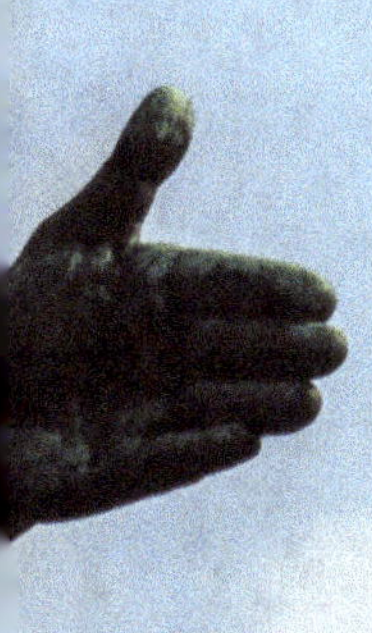

BIOGRAPHY

Lenin was born Vladimir Ilich Ulyanov. Both of his parents were well-educated and his father was a teacher. Lenin grew up attending school as an excellent student. In addition, he enjoyed playing chess as well as being outdoors.

His father died when Lenin was 16, and this angered him and he declared that he did not believe in God as well as the Russian Orthodox Church. Lenin's older brother Sacha became affiliated with a revolutionary group a year later which had plans to assassinate the Tsar. Sacha was caught and then executed by the government.

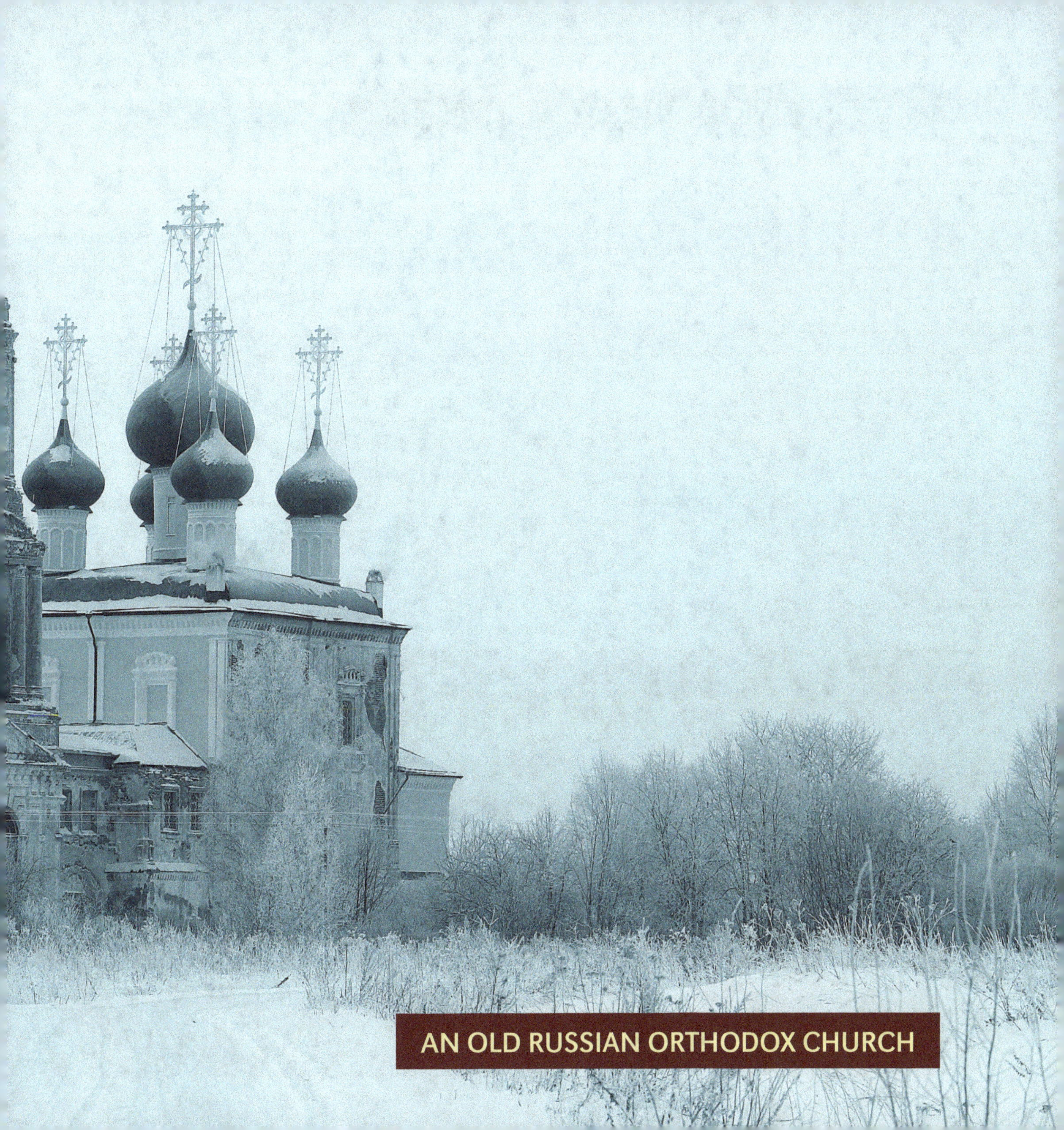
AN OLD RUSSIAN ORTHODOX CHURCH

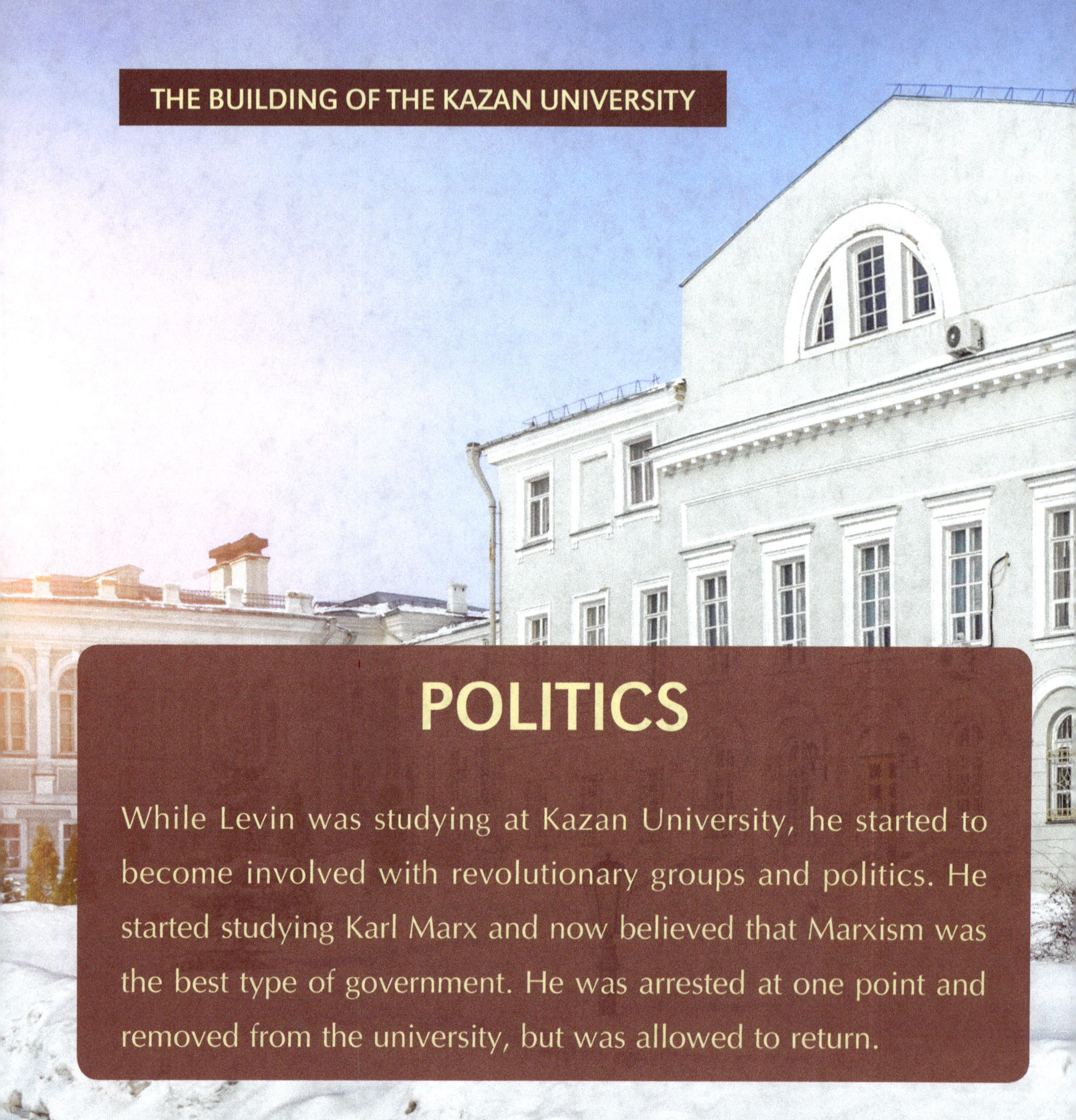

POLITICS

While Levin was studying at Kazan University, he started to become involved with revolutionary groups and politics. He started studying Karl Marx and now believed that Marxism was the best type of government. He was arrested at one point and removed from the university, but was allowed to return.

Once he graduated, he started working as a lawyer. He moved to St. Petersburg, continuing his revolutionary work, and quickly he became a Marxists leader. He was constantly having to hide from government officials and police and spies were around everywhere. Lenin eventually started the Bolsheviks, which was his own group of Marxists.

Lenin was arrested in 1897 and was exiled for three years to Siberia. Once he returned in 1900, he continued fostering his revolution and pushing Marxism. He was banned from St. Petersburg, however, and the police kept a close watch on him. During the next few years he would spend most of his time in Western Europe, writing communist papers as well as planning for the upcoming revolution.

STATUE OF VLADIMIR LENIN

In 1914, once WWI broke out, millions of Russian peasants and workmen had to join the army and were sent to battle in horrid conditions.

They would often have no food, little training, no shoes, and sometimes had to fight without any weapons. Under the Tsar leadership, millions of Russian soldiers were killed and the Russians were now ready to revolt.

FEBRUARY REVOLUTION

The February Revolution took place in Russia during 1917. The Tsar was now overthrown and the Provisional Government was now in charge of the government. With assistance from Germany, Lenin was able to return to Russia and started speaking out against this new form of government, advising that it was not any better than the Tsarist government. He wanted the people to rule the government.

РАБОЧИМ
ПУТИЛОВСКОГО
ЗАВОДА

BOLSHEVIK PARADE

BOLSHEVIK REVOLUTION

Lenin, along with his Bolshevik Party took control of the government in October of 1917. This takeover is sometimes referred to as the Bolshevik Revolution or the October Revolution. He had now established the Russian Socialist Federative Soviet Republic and was this new government's leader.

LEADER OF THE SOVIET UNION

Lenin made many changes once he established this new government. Immediately, he established peace with Germany as well as exiting WWI. Germany had been hoping for this when they assisted him in sneaking back to Russia. In addition, he absconded land from rich landholders and divided it up between the peasants.

VLADIMIR LENIN

During the first few years of his leadership, he fought in a civil war against anti-Bolsheviks. Lenin had become a brutal leader and was able to stomp out any opposition, killing anyone that would speak out against his form of government. As with the Tsar that preceded him, he made peasants join his army and took food from them to feed his solders. This war destroyed most of the economy of Russia and millions of people ended up starving to death.

Lenin created War Communism during the Russian Civil War. Under this form of government, the government would own everything and soldiers were able to take from the peasants anything they needed. After the war ended the economy was failing and Lenin established his New Economic Policy. This policy would allow some private ownership as well as capitalism, and the Russian economy was now recovering. In 1922, once the Bolsheviks had finally won this war, Lenin established the Soviet Union, which became the first communist country throughout the world.

RUSSIAN CIVIL WAR

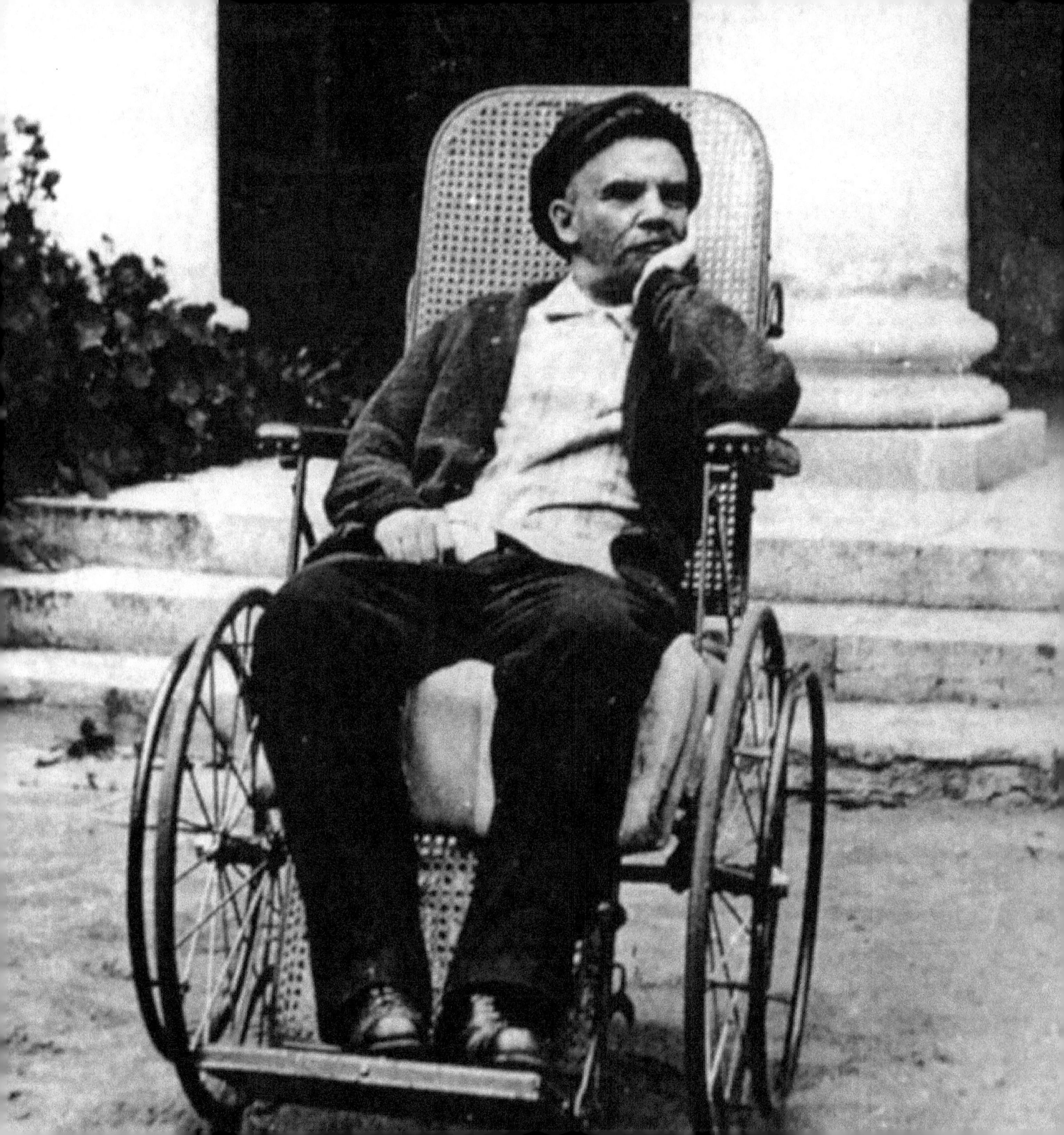

DEATH

Lenin was shot in 1918, in an attempted assassination. Even though he was able to survive, his health remained poor. He then suffered a series of strokes, beginning in 1922. On January 21, 1924, he finally passed away from another stroke.

LEGACY

Lenin will always be remembered as founder of the Soviet Union. His ideas regarding communism and Marxism are referred to as Leninism. He had become of the greatest influential political leaders during the 20th century.

RUSSIAN REVOLUTION

The Russian Revolution occurred in 1917, as peasants as well as the working-class Russians rebelled against the Tsar government. This revolution was led by Vladimir Lenin and the Bolsheviks, his team of revolutionaries. This new communist government established the Soviet Union as a country.

THE RUSSIAN TSARS

Prior to the revolution, Russia had been ruled by the Tsar, who was a powerful monarch. He would have total power over Russia, including control over the church, owning most of the land, as well as commanding the army.

RUSSIAN REVOLUTION

Life for the peasants and the working-class people was quite difficult prior to the Russian Revolution. They would often go without food, worked for little pay, as well as being exposed to unsafe working conditions. The upper class would treat the peasants like slaves, providing them with few rights and treating them just about like animals.

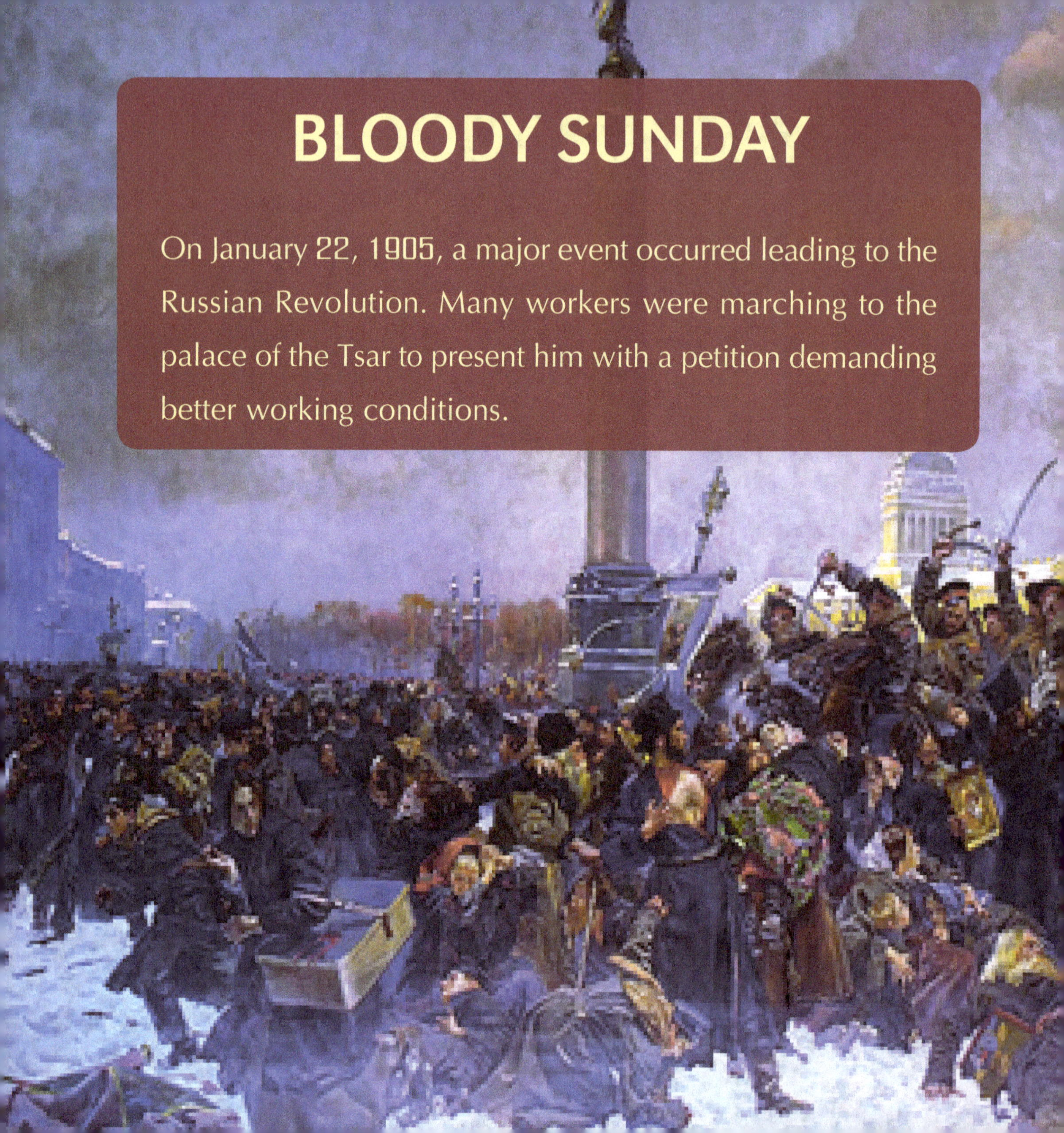

BLOODY SUNDAY

On January 22, 1905, a major event occurred leading to the Russian Revolution. Many workers were marching to the palace of the Tsar to present him with a petition demanding better working conditions.

They were then shot at by soldiers and many of them were injured or killed. This day became known as Bloody Sunday.

BLOODY SUNDAY

Prior to Bloody Sunday, most of the peasants and working-class people believed the Tsar was on their side and they revered him. They blamed the government for their troubles, not the Tsar. Following the shootings, however, the Tsar was now seen as the enemy of the working-class and the hope for revolution started to spread.

WORLD WAR I

World War I started in 1914, and Russia was now at war with Germany. A large Russian army was then created by forcing the working class and the peasant men to join the army. While the Russia army had terrific numbers, their soldiers were not trained or equipped to fight. Many were sent to battle without food, weapons, or shoes. During the following three years, almost 2 million Russian soldiers died during battle and approximately 5 million more were wounded.

WORLD WAR 1

PEACE CONFERENCE IN BREST-LITOVSK
6604

RESULTS

Russia exited WWI following the revolution by signing a peace treaty along with Germany which became known as the Treaty of Brest-Litovsk. The new government seized control over industry and moved Russia's economy from what was known to be rural to an industrial economy. Additionally, they took over farmland from the landholders and split it between the peasants. Equal rights were given to women.

Between 1918 and 1920, Russia was experiencing a civil war between the anti-Bolsheviks (also known as the White Army) and the Bolsheviks (also known as the Red Army). The Bolsheviks went on to win the war and formed the new country named USSR (United Soviet Socialist Republic).

CIVIL WAR

PETROGRAD SOVIET ASSEMBLY MEETING IN 1917

WHAT THE RED SCARE "FEARS" BROUGHT ABOUT

Though the climate of fear and repression began to ease in the late 1950s, the Red Scare has continued to influence political debate in the decades since and is often cited as an example of how unfounded fears can compromise civil liberties.

For additional on the Red Scare, you can visit your local library, research the internet, and ask questions of your teachers, family, and friends.

Visit
BABY PROFESSOR
EDUCATION KIDS
www.BabyProfessorBooks.com
to download Free Baby Professor eBooks
and view our catalog of new and exciting
Children's Books